W9-ASI-047

ALLEN PHOTOGRAPHIC GUIDES

TRAILER MAINTENANCE

CONTENTS

Compared to a car, a trailer is mechanically simple but it still needs to be serviced and maintained if it is to function properly and, most importantly, safely.

If a trailer's brakes or wheel bearings seize the wheel locks up, slewing the trailer to one side. If this happens at speed, with the horses thrown off balance, you would be very lucky if the outfit stayed upright! This is just one example of why it is so important to make sure that your horse trailer is properly maintained. The safety of you, your horses and other road users is reliant on it – as may be keeping your driving licence. Unlike some countries, Britain has no equivalent of the MOT for trailers but using an unsafe one is an offence.

IF IN DOUBT

This book should be used in conjunction with a trailer handbook because components vary even on trailers made at different times by the same manufacturer. If you do not have a handbook and find that something on your trailer differs from what you see here, do not guess but seek expert advice from the manufacturer or dealer.

Similarly, if you have any doubt about your competence to carry out a task, or are worried by anything you find, go to the experts.

If you do not have a trailer dealer in your area, a caravan dealer may be able to supply

parts and advice, though explain that it is for a horse trailer in case a more heavy duty item is required than would be used for a caravan.

EVERY-TRIP CHECKS

TYRES

As their pressures and condition are critical to trailer safety, tyres should be checked every trip. When the tyres are cold, ensure the pressures are set to those advised by the trailer manufacturer. Trailers often use much higher pressures than the average car (the Ifor Williams HB510R shown here requires 54 psi). If you cannot remember the pressures, write them on the trailer.

You must also ensure that your car's tyre pressures are correct for towing. If the handbook does not give a pressure for towing, use the one recommended for the fully laden car. If the manufacturer recommends only one pressure, regardless of load, you may find the car feels better towing with an extra 3 or 4 psi in the rear tyres, but do not

exceed the maximum marked on the tyre.

Do not forget the car and trailer spares. An electric tyre pump, powered from the car's cigarette lighter, makes topping up ten tyres much easier!

Check that the tyres have a good tread – the legal minimum is 1.6mm over the central 75 per cent of their width for the whole circumference, but anything under 3mm offers little wet road grip. If in doubt, use a tread depth gauge.

Examine the tyre walls for deep cuts or bulges: the latter means the carcass is breaking up and heading for a blowout. Look for foreign bodies in the rubber, particularly if one tyre's pressure is markedly lower than the rest.

Do not risk a trip on faulty tyres and if you have to replace any, make sure they are the size and load/speed index specified by the trailer manufacturer and therefore suitable for the trailer's maximum laden weight.

ALL RIGHT JACK

If you suffer a puncture, a wedge-type trailer lift, like the Horseware Trailerjack or Equibrand Trailer-Aid, is a safer alternative to a conventional jack. The wheel to be replaced is lifted off the ground by towing the good wheel on the same side into a recess on top of the wedge. They are safer than conventional jacks with a loaded trailer because moving horses are unlikely to rock the trailer off them.

Width in millimetres	Radial construction	Wheel diameter in inches	Max load and speed codes 89 = 580kg R = 105mph
165	**R**	**13**	**89R**

Typical tyre size, load and speed ratings moulded into the tyre wall

BODYWORK

Loose or damaged bodywork and fittings could injure you or your horse and, if they are in danger of coming off on the road or injuring other road users, they are illegal. Bits flapping about on trailers have killed people!

Make sure that top doors are properly locked back and that door and ramp catches are correctly fastened.

TOWBALL AND HITCH

The car's towball should be smeared with grease and the trailer's hitch handle should snap down easily when the ball is in place.

BREAKAWAY CABLE

It is illegal to use a braked trailer without a breakaway cable. Its job, before it snaps, is to apply the brakes if the trailer becomes unhitched, so make sure it is in good order and not attached to something on the car that may be pulled off.

LIGHTS

Every time you hitch up, ensure the trailer lights are working properly. It is easiest to get a helper to check while you work the light switches (remember the brake lights). Dampness or corrosion in the car socket or trailer plug can cause faults like lights coming on with the indicators or the opposite car and trailer indicators working together. Lamp lenses should be clean and undamaged.

STORAGE

Where you keep your trailer can make a difference to its longevity and reliability. Ideally it should be stored in a building, but few of us have buildings big enough.

Try to park it on hard standing so that it is not subject to dampness coming up from the ground. Hard standing also makes maintenance easier because it gives a firm surface for jacking it up.

Storing a trailer under trees should be avoided because their debris and sap will not enhance the exterior.

Always chock the wheels, or use a wheelclamp, and release the handbrake so that the brake shoes are not in contact with the drums. This will stop the shoes sticking to the drums while parked.

Most horse trailers have good enough ventilation to prevent condensation, but if it does start getting damp inside, open it up to dry.

SECURITY

Your trailer is always vulnerable to theft while parked so use a good security device like a wheelclamp. Hitchlocks should not be used alone because thieves have lashed trailers fitted with them to their cars. Ideally, park it where it is overlooked by houses but not easily seen from the road.

CLEANING

Never leave bedding in the trailer because it goes mouldy, which is bad for trailer and horses. Disinfecting after every trip, as professional transporters must, may be excessive for private use but washing it out keeps germs and moulds at bay. Leave it open to dry out.

Externally, try to prevent mud building up in nooks and crannies because it absorbs road salt and becomes a corrosive poultice, as well as making it harder to see if rot sets in.

A power washer is useful for cleaning trailers inside and out but even domestic ones can produce a 1500psi jet of water, so be careful not to force water into places you do not want it.

WHEELS

If you do not use your trailer for very long periods (like all winter) it is sensible to remove the wheels and store them under cover to protect the tyres from the effects of weather and ultraviolet light. You can leave the trailer on blocks or axle stands or buy 'winter wheels' from a caravan dealer, which are stands bolted on in place of the wheels, often with locking devices.

If you store your trailer with the wheels on you should move it about once a month so that the tyres do not get flat spots – just moving the trailer a foot or so is enough.

GENERAL MAINTENANCE

HEALTH AND SAFETY

⚠️ **WARNING!** Working on trailers can be dangerous. When preparing to work on your trailer, always ensure that you follow these points for safety and protection.

Never work under a trailer raised on a jack alone because jacks often collapse, so use axle stands. Always ensure that the ground under a jack or stand is firm enough to take the weight. If you have to put something under the stand or jack, use blocks of wood. Never use house bricks which split too easily and without warning.

When jacking up a trailer use an axle or a substantial part of the chassis as a jacking point, never use the floor.

Wear eye protection when working under any vehicle because you can easily dislodge potentially damaging dirt. For greasy jobs, use a barrier cream on your hands and clean them using a suitable hand cleaner, like Swarfega or Manista. If you have sensitive skin, thin latex gloves like surgeons use are essential when handling grease.

If you do not have the correct equipment to do the job properly and safely either leave it until you can buy them or get a dealer to do it.

BODYWORK

The materials used in trailer bodies vary from make to make and most handbooks explain the care required. Modern composites need little attention. Wood should be kept as dry as possible and checked for rot, though beware of using wood preservatives on plywood in case it affects the glue bonding the layers together.

Steel needs attention if minor damage is not to become a major rust problem. A dab of paint on a small scratch as soon as it happens prevents a rust spot forming to eventually spread under surrounding paint. If the steel is already rusty, you must remove the rust with emery paper or a wire brush before repainting, though anti-corrosion paints, like Hammerite, only need loose rust flakes removed.

The galvanised coating of some metals is self-healing over small areas of damage but larger scrapes should be painted over with a zinc-rich paint, like Holts Zinc Plate.

BOLTS

These days bolts at critical points are usually self-locking, but their security – particularly of those securing axles, springs and hitch – should still be checked every 2000 miles.

BRAKES

Trailers have overrun brakes where the hitch pushing against the slowing towcar operates the drum brakes at each wheel via rods and cables. Unlike most modern cars, trailer brakes are not self-adjusting so they need to be adjusted for wear according to manufacturers' recommendations.

Adjustment is normally done after about 500 miles on a new trailer, or after fitting new brake shoes, and then at 2500 to 3000 miles. Before adjusting the brakes, check the operating cables are undamaged – kinked or broken ones should be replaced.

⚠️ **DANGER!** Brakes are essential to road safety so if you have any doubts about your ability to work on them, or about anything you find on them, seek your trailer dealer's advice.

1. Jack the trailer up and put it on axle stands so that all four wheels are off the ground.
2. Ensure the handbrake is off and the hitch is pulled fully forwards.
3. Rotate the wheel in the direction of forward travel while turning the adjuster nut on the back plate of the drum until the brakes are applied. Do not rotate the wheel in the reverse direction or the auto-reverse mechanism releases the brakes.
4. Now gradually turn the nut the other way until the wheel just rotates again. The nut does not have to be turned far.

5. Older trailers may have a star-wheel adjuster inside the drum. This is accessed by removing a plastic bung in the back plate and is turned with a screwdriver blade, but adjustment is otherwise the same as with a nut adjuster.

6. Apply the handbrake a couple of times to centre the shoes, then recheck the wheel and make any final adjustments. Do all the other wheels.

7. To check for correct adjustment, take hold of a brake cable where it comes out of its outer sheath at the compensator bar. With your thumbnail against the end of the sheath, you should be able to pull the cable out by 3mm to 5mm.

The cables do not normally need adjustment, but should be checked. There should be no more than about 1mm of play between the hitch draw tube (see hitches on page 13) and the main brake operating lever it pushes against. With all the brakes adjusted at the drums, you can check cable adjustment by applying the handbrake and turning each wheel in the reverse direction: each should click and lock. If there is too much slack in the cables, the handbrake will come all the way up and the last wheel will not lock.

Adjustment is made by turning adjuster nuts on the main rod or cable connecting the lever to the compensating bar under the trailer to which the individual wheel cables attach.

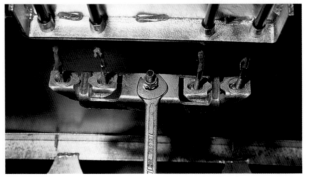

The brake cables to the wheels should all be the same length, which can be checked by measuring the distance between the compensator bar and a chassis crossmember. If a cable appears to have stretched, it should be replaced and others checked – a job best done by a dealer.

Once you are sure you have adjusted the brakes properly, do a road test on a safe road. When you brake firmly the trailer should pull up evenly and straight. When you reverse, the brakes should come off but if they do not, you have adjusted the shoes and/or the rod too tightly and they should be readjusted .

Note: many pre-1989 trailers have a lever to disable the brakes for reversing instead of the safer auto-reverse mechanism.

FLOORS

Lift rubber matting regularly to clean underneath it and allow any dampness to dry out. Worn rubber matting must be replaced to protect the floor and to ensure the horses have a safe, slip-resistant footing.

Examine the floor from above and below for any signs of rot or damage. Floors must be repaired by a trailer dealer who knows the correct materials to use – a horse trailer floor takes a lot of weight and stress and getting it wrong could be disastrous.

Granular rubber compounds that look like tarmac are occasionally used on trailer floors instead of rubber sheeting. This provides a permanent slip-resistant surface but any moisture seeping in around the trailer sides or floor-mounted fittings cannot get out again and you cannot inspect the wood below for damage.

HINGES AND CATCHES

Occasionally oil hinges and catches to prevent wear and ensure they work smoothly and quietly – a nervous horse will not appreciate a ramp that squeals. If you find ordinary oil makes dust stick, try WD40. A smear of grease on the lugs that ramp counterbalance springs hook onto stops them 'twanging' as it rises.

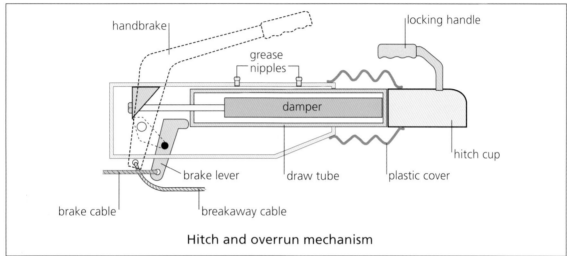

Hitch and overrun mechanism

HITCHES AND TOWBALLS

The hitch does more than just hold the trailer onto the car, it is part of the braking system. The hitch cup is bolted to a sliding tube, called the draw tube, which applies the brakes when it is pushed back by the trailer coming forwards as the towcar brakes. All trailers have at least one grease nipple on top of the housing for this tube and most have two. A few also have one underneath to lubricate the pivot of the lever the tube pushes against.

Most manufacturers recommend using a grease gun to push grease through these nipples at between 2000 and 3000 miles. At the same time, push the hitch backwards: it should slide steadily back under firm pressure and when released it should slide steadily out again. If it offers little resistance to being pushed back or comes back out quickly, the damper inside (like a gas strut) has failed. If it stays back, and a dose of grease through the grease nipples does not cure it, the damper has stuck or the drawtube is damaged. In both cases it should be corrected as soon as possible, because it affects braking efficiency, and the work is best carried out by an expert who is properly able to assess damage.

Grease and dirt in the hitch cup should be cleaned out at the same intervals (every 2000–3000 miles) with white spirit on a paintbrush – more often if you tow on dirt tracks – or the combination of grit and grease act like grinding paste on the hitch and towball. Once dry, wipe a smear of grease inside the cup. All moving hitch parts should be kept oiled.

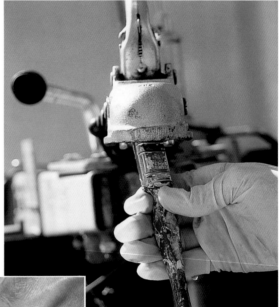

Worn hitches and towballs can be dangerous, so get them checked – garages can measure towballs when the car is serviced. Putting a new trailer onto an old towball accelerates wear so if you buy a new trailer or hitch, spend a few pounds on a new towball and bolts too.

LIGHTS

Trailer electrics are simple but are subject to a great deal of spray thrown up by the towcar's wheels, so investigate any malfunctions immediately. Stopping a lamp leaking as soon as you notice it may save having to replace it later or having it fail.

A problem with more than one light suggests a wiring fault in the car or trailer. You can check which by plugging the trailer into another car's socket – if the problem disappears, your car is at fault. The trailer plug and car socket are the most likely places for faults, so start your check there.

Every 2000 miles, or every six months, examine the contacts in the trailer electrical plug and car socket and clean off corrosion and dirt (insects often get squashed deep between the pins). A Hella Kleenaplug, available from caravan dealers, makes the job easier and a squirt of WD40 helps prevent corrosion.

At the same time, remove the lamp lenses and check the contacts and bulb holders for corrosion. Some lamps have drain holes in them which must be kept clear. Also, wipe out any dirt on the inside of the lens and give the contacts (but not the bulb glass) a squirt of WD40. Damaged lenses or badly corroded fittings should be replaced.

Finally, check the cable runs for damage to the insulation by vermin or abrasion. The cable between the plug and the trailer is most vulnerable.

⚠ **DANGER!** Make sure the trailer is disconnected from the car before working on its electrics. When cleaning the car's towing socket turn off the ignition and lights and remove the key.

RAMPS

Most trailers have some form of lifting assistance on at least the large rear ramp. This is usually a spring and can sometimes be adjusted to compensate for wear by turning a nut or bolt, but in some cases the only answer may be to replace the spring. Only adjust the spring until you can lift the ramp easily and not so much that it refuses to stay down.

Some trailers have gas struts on ramps. If these fail, or get bent, they cannot be repaired and must be replaced.

DANGER! Never take a gas strut apart, or puncture one, because they contain gas at high pressure.

Check the condition of the ramp itself because a horse going through a rotten one can seriously injure himself. Some ramps give a little as the horse walks on, but if it flexes more than usual, or excessively, it should be investigated.

WHEELNUTS

On a new trailer, or if you have to remove a wheel, you should check the tightness of the wheelnuts after the first 25 miles (you should also do this on cars). After that their tightness should be checked every 500 miles or so.

Some trailer manufacturers give a torque wrench setting for wheelnuts which, if you have the tool, is more sensible than brute force. Never exert excessive force on a wheel brace because you may not be able to undo the nuts later and you can damage the threads. A smear of anti-seize grease (like Comma Copper Ease) on the threads stops nuts locking on.

Wheel nuts on cars and trailers should be tightened in diagonal pairs to pull the wheel evenly onto the hub.

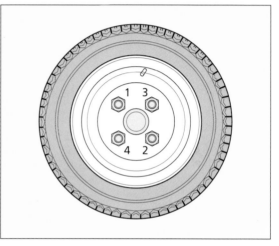

SERVICING AXLES

DANGER! The items in this section are vital for road safety so if you have any doubts about your ability to do the work properly, get your trailer dealer to do it.

Some of the latest trailers, especially those from Ifor Williams, have wheel bearings that are sealed for life, like modern cars, and so need no adjustment or regreasing.

Instead of a slotted (castle) nut and split pin behind the hub cap most of these have a stake nut, which has a collar projecting from it for locking the nut by tapping the metal into a groove on the axle (staking). Each time the drum is removed, the stake nut usually has to be replaced and tightened

to a specific torque setting (350 Newton metres on an Ifor Williams) for which a large torque wrench is essential. Any work on drums and hubs on these trailers is best left to a dealer.

REMOVING THE DRUM

⚠ **DANGER!** This applies only to axles with a slotted nut and split pin – not sealed-for-life hubs.

1. Loosen the wheelnuts to finger tightness then either put the trailer on axle stands, so that all four wheels are off the ground, or lift one wheel at a time and chock the others. Release the handbrake and check the hitch is pulled fully forwards.

2. Remove the hub cap. You are supposed to be able to lever them off with a screwdriver but metal ones often need tapping off with a hammer and large screwdriver or small cold chisel used evenly around the flange. Clean the grease out of the cap and put the part somewhere safe and clean.

3. Clean the grease away to reveal the slotted nut and split pin. Straighten out the ends of the split pin and pull or tap it out – this will be replaced, so discard the old one after checking that your new one is the same diameter and length.

4. Turn the nut anti-clockwise to undo it and put it somewhere safe and clean.

5. Slacken the brake adjuster nut or star wheel right off (see pages 10–11). You should now be able to remove the drum by pulling it towards you, though you may need to tap it gently around its back edge with a mallet or a piece of wood and hammer. The outer wheel bearing often falls out as the drum is pulled off, so be ready to catch it!

You are now ready to work on the wheel bearings or brakes.

DANGER! Do not inhale brake dust because it may contain asbestos and even asbestos-free dust is an irritant. Never blow it away by mouth or air line but use a proprietary brake cleaner or a damp cloth to remove it.

GREASING WHEEL BEARINGS

The wheel bearings are two sets of roller bearings which prevent friction between the wheel hub, which is in the centre of the brake drum, and the axle on which it turns. Check the bearings at least annually and regrease every two years – more often if mileage is high or you drive in dusty conditions.

1. Note how the bearings and grease seal are fitted. As mentioned, the outer bearing normally falls out as you slide the drum off so be ready to catch it. Place the hub outer side down and lever the grease seal out – it is sensible to replace this but not essential unless damaged or worn.
2. Lift the inner bearing out of the hub and wipe the grease off both bearings and the hub. If the grease appears contaminated – or if you drop a bearing in the dirt – clean it off using white spirit, petrol or paraffin. Check for wear and get a new one if necessary.
3. Push grease down into the gap between the inner and outer rings of the bearing, but do not pack it too tightly. Use a heat resistant grease suitable for wheel bearings, like LM grease.
4. Refit the inner bearing to the hub, taking care not to get grease on the inside of the drum or it will ruin the brake linings. Fit the grease seal by putting a flat piece of wood over it (here a purpose made tool is being used) and tapping it with a hammer, ensuring that it is pushed in evenly to its original position. Turn it over and fit the outer bearing.

Now go on to the section on refitting and adjusting the hub on page 22.

BRAKE SHOE REPLACEMENT

⚠ **DANGER!** Brake dust may contain asbestos. If you get grease onto the friction surfaces of the shoes or inside the brake drum, clean it off thoroughly with a solvent. Shoes must always be replaced on both wheels on an axle or the trailer will pull to one side when braking.

On most brakes you can check the amount of friction material left on the shoes through a hole in the back plate covered by a plastic bung. Manufacturers usually suggest replacement when the material is down to 1.5mm.

Before you start taking the brake components apart, familiarise yourself with how they are fitted, drawing a diagram if necessary. Note if the shoes are an asymmetric shape, if one spring is longer than the other and which way the hooks on the spring ends face. Compare your new parts with those fitted and set up the new shoes and springs to one side using the originals as a pattern. Brake shoes can usually only be fitted the correct way round, but do not rely on that!

As you work on the brakes look for signs of wear or corrosion – replacing a rusty spring now will save work later.

You replace the shoes with the brake adjuster fully slackened off, so check the shoe ends are resting on the adjuster's housing.

1. Release the shoe-retaining spring, or springs, by compressing it from inside the brake and unhooking it from behind the drum's back plate. Some have tiny metal inserts to retain the spring.

2. Lift the upper and lower shoes and their springs out together by spreading the ends over the adjuster. If there are two springs between the shoes, you may need to lever the shoes apart with a screwdriver or spanner to lift them off the adjuster. If your new shoes do not come with new springs, transfer the old ones to them now while you can see the existing positions.

3. Remove the expander mechanism the brake cable is attached to and check it for wear and freedom of movement.

4. Take hold of the end of the cable in a pair of pliers and check it moves easily and smoothly. If it does not, it should be replaced.

5. Remove and clean the brake adjuster nut or star wheel, unscrewing it to make sure it is not stuck or corroded.

6. Ensure the other adjuster parts move freely. They often stick.

Steps 7 to 11 continue on page 22

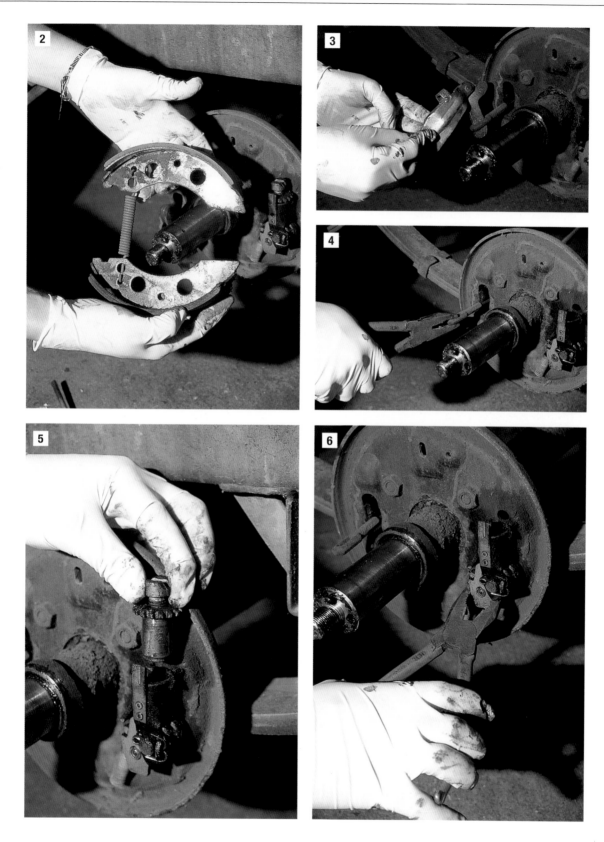

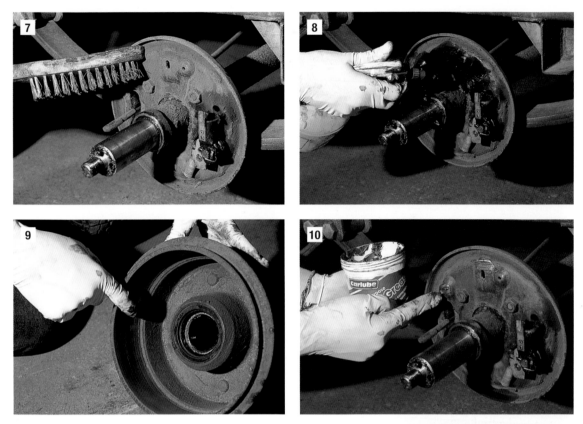

7. Carefully clean any rust and grime off the back plate with a wire brush – do not be tempted to blow it away!

8. Clean the backplate and inside the drum with a proprietary brake cleaner and leave it to dry.

9. Check the drum braking surface for any deep scoring. If it is scored, the drum should be replaced – unlike car drums, those on trailers are not usually thick enough for 'skimming'.

10. Carefully put a smear of heat resistant copperised grease (like Comma Copper Ease) onto the points on the back plate, levers and adjuster touched by the shoe but make sure none gets onto the friction surfaces.

11. Reassemble the brake in the reverse order, ensuring that the expander mechanism lever to which the cable is attached sits in this position so that it is not applying the brake.

You are now ready to refit the hub and adjust it and should then adjust the brakes as explained on page 10.

REFITTING THE HUB

Once you are satisfied your work inside the brake drum and hub is finished, carefully refit the drum over the end of the axle, being careful not to push the bearings out of place. Some people find it easier to slip the outer bearing in after the drum has been put onto the axle but, if you can hold it there with your thumbs, it is easier to get correct alignment by having it in place.

You may need to tap the drum gently with a mallet or piece of wood and hammer to get it fully home, while checking that the brake shoes are properly aligned. Do not force it! Replace the slotted nut finger tight then put the wheel onto the hub, doing the nuts up finger tight.

HUB ADJUSTMENT

Some manufacturers require the adjustment of the hub nuts to be checked after the new trailer's first 500 to 1200 miles. It must also be done if the hub is removed to work on the brakes or bearings. Note that rocking the wheel is not a check of whether bearings need adjustment because, on a trailer, the bearing needs play to allow for heat expansion.

Some details of adjustment may vary from trailer to trailer, so check with the manufacturer. For example, in step one the hub nut may need turning back anything from 30 to 90 degrees.

1. While turning the wheel, tighten the nut until resistance is felt, then turn the nut back until the wheel turns freely.

⚠ DANGER! Overtightening the nut damages the bearings.

2. Insert a new split pin by aligning the nearest nut slot to the hole in the axle. You may need to gently tap it home.
3. Bend the ends of the pin apart with a screwdriver blade or pliers then tap the outer one back flat over the end of the axle and the inner one down against the side of the nut.
4. Check the pin ends are not sticking out or interfering with moving parts. Put a little clean grease into the hub cap and tap it back into place with a mallet or wood and hammer.

When you have finished all the work and lowered the trailer, tighten all the wheel nuts (see page 17). Road test the trailer, making sure it brakes evenly and straight. Also feel the hub centres and examine any that feel warmer than the others.

ACKNOWLEDGEMENTS

My thanks to: Mid Norfolk Canopies and Trailers, Scarning, Dereham, Norfolk NR19 2PG, for help with photos and advice; Peter Leslie of Ifor Williams Trailers, Cynwyd Corwen, Denbighshire, for advice and a very long phone call; Safe and Secure Products, Wick, near Bristol, for the picture of their winter wheels; Rice Trailers, Bateson Trailers, Pegasus Trailers UK and Avonride (trailer hitch and axle makers) for information on their products.

British Library Cataloguing-in-Publication Data.
A catalogue record for this book is available from the British Library

ISBN 0.85131.752.9

© J. A. Allen 1999

Published in Great Britain in 1999 by
J. A. Allen an imprint of Robert Hale Ltd.,
Clerkenwell House, 45–47 Clerkenwell Green,
London EC1R 0HT

Design and Typesetting by Paul Saunders
Series editor Jane Lake
Colour processing by Tenon & Polert Colour Processing Ltd., Hong Kong
Printed in Hong Kong by Dah Hua International Printing Press Co. Ltd.